"In Memory of my wife Shirley for her love and devotion to her family and friends".

A SENIOR'S EXPERIENCES AND OBSERVATIONS

Moving, Health, Caregiving & Conflicts

E. GRANT REES

Order this book online at www.trafford.com
or email orders@trafford.com

Most Trafford titles are also available at major online book retailers.

© Copyright 2016 E. Grant Rees.

Print information available on the last page.

ISBN: 978-1-4907-6945-5 (sc)
ISBN: 978-1-4907-6947-9 (hc)
ISBN: 978-1-4907-6946-2 (e)

Library of Congress Control Number: 2016901552

Trafford rev. 01/28/2016

www.trafford.com

North America & international
toll-free: 1 888 232 4444 (USA & Canada)
fax: 812 355 4082

INTRODUCTION

MY WIFE AND I HAVE always been active. We have traveled with family and friends, camped with family in tents, and later with a Coleman camp trailer. Our family skied at Mount Hood in Oregon, Blue Knob in Pennsylvania, the Grand Tetons in Wyoming, Kelly Canyon and Sun Valley in Idaho; and Alta, Snowbird, Brighton, Park City, and Beaver Mountain in Utah. We took our family on many trips. Since we lived in various locations (California, Oregon, Maryland, Idaho, and now Utah) our family was able to visit many historical sites, national parks, museums, and various landscapes. When we became "empty nesters", we joined a group that met twice monthly for games and scripture-related study. We also traveled with other friends on several cruises including the Panama Canal, Hawaii, Alaska, Mexican Riviera, and Eastern & Western Caribbean. We also went golfing and bowling, but not too often.

But age finally caught up with us! Our travel and physical activities became limited. We were able to attend a water aerobics class that helped keep our joints from "rusting", and at the same time enjoy conversations with others who attend the classes. Over the years we have had various surgeries that have slowed us down.

Life's challenges become more difficult with age, especially those older than 60 years of age who I'll call "seniors". These challenges include health issues, moving, getting good medical care, caregiving, and coping with various forms of stress. The following chapters discuss these problems including personal experiences with the medical and health care systems, experiences as a caregiver, and the stress caused by all of the political conflicts and scandals as the world around us is changing at an accelerating pace. I have found that these stresses are particularly difficult for me as well as my senior friends. The honesty and trust of people, including government and medical personnel, lawyers, and the public in general all come to mind and becomes overwhelming at times when it seems that the situations are getting worse, and not being resolved.

It is hoped that the information presented herein will help others when faced with similar issues.

The photo of Shirley on the front cover was taken in July, 2006 at Yellowstone Bear World, located five miles south of Rexburg, Idaho.

CONTENTS

———— ✒ ✒ ————

CHAPTER ONE

————— ✿ ✿ —————

MOVING PROBLEMS FOR SENIORS

MANY OF OUR FRIENDS HAVE died or are requiring help from others, including their families.

Thus we started to plan for a different life style. Growing older and having health issues from time to time, my wife and I decided to move closer to our family. Family members had to travel relatively long distances to visit us when we were in the hospital or not feeling well. Thus we contemplated moving.

We looked at various locations and considered different types of housing. Our homes have been split level, colonial style with all bedrooms on the 2nd floor and laundry in the basement, and ranch style homes with basements. As we get older and have difficulty walking, using stairs in multiple level homes is an additional challenge.

Some seniors want to move to a senior living facility The living facilities are usually small apartments with one or two bedrooms with limited area for clothes, a living room for a small kitchen table, a couch, a TV, and a small desk. A portion of a wall is usually designed as a "kitchen". Most of these small "apartments" do not have a laundry room within the individual units and one has to use a community laundry room down the hall. Usually there are no covered areas or garage for your vehicle. Some seniors may need to move to an assisted living facility if family members are not able to assist or such a living environment would make life more enjoyable by associating with others. In either case this means getting rid of many household items, and most people just don't want to part with anything. Excess clothing, furniture, and other items need to be disposed of or put in storage that generally means paying storage fees for items that likely will never be used or even seen again! The advantages of these living facilities include meals, activities, and transportation to shopping centers or doctor appointments. Those who have the ability to scale-down to the bare essentials are free to relax in these facilities and can focus on enjoying the rest of their lives, including friends, TV, movies (DVDs), their photo albums and updating their personal journals and family history.

We were not ready for a senior living facility so we decided to move into a senior development designed for persons 55 years of age or older. These homes are single level and some have basements. We found a development to our liking in Utah where one of our sons lives. The home owners association has strict covenants that does not permit pets of any kind. At that time we had a dog, a dachshund we named "Keesha", which was fourteen years old. Our veterinarian told us that our dog was experiencing kidney failure and estimated that the dog's life expectancy was less than six months. This dog was our third dachshund. When the first one died ("Poco"), we got a second one, "Buster". They were good pets and gave us comfort. It was especially hard for my wife to accept not getting another dog, one that would likely outlive us, and we were concerned who would care for the dog when we could no longer do so. One of our sons & wife were not interested in that responsibility, and our other son already had a dog. Also, we were getting older and cleaning up after the dog outside would be much harder, one reason being that the association's covenants did not allow fences between lots, and if they did, the costs for lawn care would increase dramatically.

After a few months a home in this senior development became available. We were concerned with how much "scaling-down" of our "stuff" would be necessary. We surmised that we would not have to dispose of very much if we added additional storage shelves and did some re-modeling. Then, in 2009, we bought the home and proceeded to make improvements. We moved the bulk of our furniture while doing some remodeling, and when our dog died we moved into our newly acquired home.

After moving in my wife proclaimed that this was our last move! I agreed with her. But now, about six years later, we found some neighbors had to move into nursing homes or assisted-living facilities. Now, more than ever I really think we ought to "scale-down". If we could not care for one another any longer, we would be leaving a house full of "stuff" and a lot of work and decisions for our family at a time when they are all busy. There can be much joy when we make the decision to give out possessions to others, and know that they are appreciated and used.

I cannot understand the rationale to keep things that are not used. Some people pay storage fees for items for years, and they cannot remember what they stored! How sad! We need to formulate criteria for keeping "stuff": if we have not worn or used something in the past three years, it should be a candidate for immediate disposal -- sell or give it away. Easy to say, hard for some people to do, or procrastinate doing it!

The old scout motto ("be prepared") comes to mind that we should prepare for the future by "downscaling" because of the eventual possibly of needing to move to a nursing home or an assisted living facility. In that case I would not want to leave a house full of furniture, clothing, etc. which I may never be able to see or use again.

CHAPTER TWO

—⁂—

FINDING AND SELECTING A DOCTOR

IN MOVING TO A NEW community, we are faced with selecting our doctors. This task takes some thought and methodology.

For years my wife had a bad shoulder and her orthopedic surgeons told her that she needed a total shoulder replacement to relieve the pain, but the surgery would not give her any more motion than she had before the surgery. She could not raise her arm any higher than her waist and after some inquiries we could not find any success stories of total shoulder replacements. So she lived with a bad shoulder for several years.

When we were contemplating moving near our son in Utah, he told us of a specialty hospital which performed for all types of orthopedic surgeries. We conferred with newly acquired friends, and made some calls to various doctor offices and asked questions. We created a list of possible surgeons for a total shoulder replacement. After checking out these doctors on-line and asking a few people, we narrowed our list. After hearing of some success stories of this type of surgery, we made an appointment with our choice for a surgeon. We were impressed and set a date for the surgery.

The surgery was successful. A week or so after the surgery I went with my wife to her appointment with the surgeon. I asked the surgeon about the range of motion my wife might experience with her new shoulder. He said that after physical therapy she would have full range of motion, lifting his hand high in the air and then to the back of his neck. After some weeks of physical therapy, Shirley did experience this range of motion!

While in the process of finding an orthopedic surgeon, we were also searching for a family or an internal medicine doctor, an eye doctor, and others.

My wife's friend, Marcia, was a nurse. She always maintained a list of doctors whom she would contact if she needed one. Whenever she traveled, she would add doctors' names to her list. She always knew a few recommended orthopedic surgeons wherever she went skiing. She was a surgical nurse and could evaluate various surgeons, and in speaking with her colleagues she could confirm her list.

Nurses and other medical staff personnel are great sources of information, but their job could be in jeopardy if they talk too much. Shirley's sister, Barbara, is a retired nurse and always has good doctors; however, she lives in another State and has no contacts or knowledge of doctors in our area.

After a while living in a new community we met new friends in our neighborhood, at our church, and at a health spa where we attended an aquatic class. When the opportunity arose, we would ask questions relative to doctors in the area. Knowing that we were newcomers, these new friends were willing to give us suggestions or comments. Our son also had some suggestions. Patients, friends and medical personnel are good sources of information.

With the federal government now taking over the medical profession, we are told that "we can keep our doctor", but the question not being asked is "what choice do we have if we need a new doctor?" Thus, in the future, we may not have a choice in choosing a doctor, the choice will be made for us. All doctors will have the same number of patients – that's only fair – no rewards for being the best and no incentive for doctors to do better!

During a conversation with a doctor in our church, I told him that we needed to find a doctor. He immediately recommended one, and without any further inquiry, I made an appointment to visit the internal medicine doctor. My first impression was good, and shortly afterwards Shirley selected the same doctor.

For a number years my wife had been taking the blood-thinning medication warfarin (Coumadin), and needed to have her blood tested periodically. I was not concerned with her medications and did not pay any attention to her tests. But after we moved and she had a new doctor I became aware of some of her medications and the blood test, Pro Time (prothrombin time) which measures how quickly the blood clots and is given as an International Normalized Ratio (INR). I was surprised that she had to go to the doctor's office either every week or every other week to have this test.

During my Navy career, I was required to have an annual physical. It was a well-organized physical. A few weeks before the visit with a doctor, I was scheduled for eye and hearing tests. Blood was drawn and a urine sample was provided for laboratory tests, and blood pressure & body weight were recorded. Depending on my age, a chest X-ray and/ or an EKG would also be done. Thus at the appointed time, the doctor had all of the laboratory data and then would examine my body: check for hernias, examine ears, mouth, skin, reflexes, listen to my lungs and heart, etc. After a thorough examination, the doctor would then counsel me concerning any problems including weight control, nutrition, vision, hearing, etc.

As a young naval officer I was assigned to the engineering department aboard a navy destroyer. The vertical ladders to the engine and fire rooms caused me to have a double hernia, probably because as a young boy I had a weakness and I recall wearing a strap for a year or two. I had a double hernia operation at a naval hospital in Sasebo, Japan on 11 December 1961. Less than a year later it reoccurred on the left side, thus another surgery done aboard the Hospital ship, USS Haven (AH-12) on 6 November 1962. About nine years later after finishing a tour in Vietnam I was reassigned to Portland, Oregon as the Resident Supervisor of Shipbuilding at which time I had another hernia. I had met several medical students and residents at our church. I asked them if they could recommend a surgeon, and they all recommended the same surgeon, a young doctor who was respected for his skills in the operating room. Since there were no Navy hospitals close to Portland at that time, I got permission to have my surgery done at the civilian hospital in Portland and I was able to get the recommended surgeon to perform the operation in 1970. I have never had any problem with a hernia since that time.

After retiring from the Navy, I worked as an engineer and the company had almost the same annual medical exam format as I had experienced in the Navy. I have often thought that such a medical exam format would be a good idea for every adult every year or two.

As a youth I observed that most doctors had their own private offices and visits to the doctors were infrequent for most people. Now my doctors want to see me every three months, probably more to do with insurance coverage and payments than with the patient's requirement to see the doctor that often. Just a few years ago my internal medicine doctor would check my skin and if he thought it might be pre-cancer, he would zap it with liquid nitrogen. But now you are referred to a dermatologist. The different medical disciplines seem to be hired by large medical corporations, and then they refer patients to see other doctors, or for lab work; thus it appears that these medical doctors and other medical providers share in the profits of the corporation. Some believe that doctors prescribe many tests and procedures in order to minimize the probability of a lawsuit, while others believe that it for the purpose of boosting medical corporate profits, especially if the patient has good medical insurance coverage.

When a procedure or test is prescribed, the patient is never told the cost if it is covered by insurance. The cost of prescriptions is expensive, and those without insurance are sometimes given some sample drugs.

With all of the drugs being prescribed, I wonder if the doctor gets a few gratuities from the drug companies.

Most of the doctor visits could be handled on the phone! The doctor listens to your lungs and heart with a stethoscope through your clothes, a practice not observed in my younger years. The doctor reviews your prescriptions and in ten minutes you are through, although you might have waited a half hour or longer in the waiting rooms. The doctor does not look in your mouth, check reflexes, etc. I sometimes think that internal medicine doctors are pharmacists with a stethoscope hanging around their necks.

After a year or so with our internal medicine doctor Shirley expressed the feeling that the doctor did not like older people! I didn't think much about these comments until much later. Could my wife's intuition be right? We shall see!

CHAPTER THREE

A DIAGNOSTIC SURPRISE

I HAD A ROUTINE VISIT with my internal medicine doctor in August of 2010. I had a cough for a few weeks. The doctor said that he heard some sounds in my lungs, and ordered a chest x-ray and a CT Scan. After a few days the doctor called me with some bad news: I had Pulmonary Fibrosis. The doctor's office made an appointment with a specialist in Ogden, a town thirty miles away. I was told that there was no cure or treatment for Pulmonary Fibrosis.

The specialist suggested that I move to Sea level and that I walk for an hour each day. The doctor prescribed Prednisone 20 mg, and suggested that I also take Calcium plus Vitamin D. The doctor told me that prednisone seemed to be effective on 20% of his patients.

Then the doctor showed me the x-rays and informed me that one of the nerves to my diaphragm had been severed. This was my "diagnostic surprise"! This had occurred when I had neck surgery in 2003. **I had not known this before.** I'm not sure that this had anything to do with me getting pulmonary fibrosis. In October, 2010, the doctor also prescribed oxygen at night.

At this point I did not know anything about Pulmonary Fibrosis, or the nerves to the diaphragm. This was the start of my searching various websites about medical conditions, medications, and terms. The diagnosis was "idiopathic pulmonary fibrosis"; "Idiopathic" means no cause has been found.

The **phrenic nerves** originate in the neck (C3-C5) and passes down between the lung and heart to reach the diaphragm. It is important for breathing, as it passes motor information to the diaphragm and receives sensory information from it. **There are two phrenic nerves, a left and a right one.** Severing a phrenic nerve paralyzes that half of the diaphragm and makes breathing more difficult, but lung function will continue provided the other nerve is intact.

After I filled the prescription for Prednisone, I chose NOT to take it for a number of reasons. After researching on the web I learned that the drug suppresses the immune system and patients are susceptible to infections. If it appeared effective on 20%, of the doctor's patients, I was wondering what serious consequences were experienced by the other 80%; and of the 20%, how much longer did they live.

When you submit to chemo and other medicines that affect your immune system, one never knows what condition needs to be treated next, and that means more medications!

Current treatments for pulmonary fibrosis are aimed at preventing more scarring of the lung, but they cannot remove any scarring. The use of oxygen can prevent pulmonary hypertension. Prednisone is prescribed to reduce inflammation, but can have serious side effects. This drug may help prevent further scarring and increase survival time in some patients, but they don't work for everyone with pulmonary fibrosis. The course of idiopathic pulmonary fibrosis is very difficult to predict; however, the average life expectancy is two to five years, depending on the rate of deterioration. One statistic indicated the median life span for this disease after diagnosis is 2.8 years!

Learning this, I immediately made plans for my "departure" and prepared check list files for my wife and turned over the monthly finances to her, which we have shared all of our married life. I also hurriedly wrote a small book discussing several years of my political thoughts which was published in 2011 as *"Can We? Comments and Recommendations for Preserving Our Nation"*.

Later, in August of 2010, I decided to seek a second medical opinion. I made an appointment with another doctor in Salt Lake City. I discovered that he was more interested that I participate in one of the research studies with the University of Utah than prescribing any treatment. He referred my name to the cognizant personnel at the University. I talked to them and found that all of the study medicines would affect my immune system. I started to wonder whether I would be any better off by participating in the tests. I also thought that maybe I should participate in a study for benefit of medical science and research.

I was informed that four studies were being conducted at the Lung Health Research Center for Idiopathic Pulmonary Fibrosis (IPF): 1) The PANTHER trial, 2) the ACE Trial, 3) The CENTOCOR trial, and 4) The ARTEMIS trial. All of these trials have serious side effects. After considering the frequent long trips to the University and the potential side effects, I decided not to participate.

The **PANTHER-IPF TRIAL** was the first trial to test the safety and effectiveness of the combination therapy of **prednisone**, azathioprine, and N-acetylcysteine (NAC). The first two drugs help suppress inflammation, and NAC can slow the growth of the scar tissue.

The **ACE TRIAL** was a controlled study to assess whether **warfarin** would do the following: 1) increase length of time between hospitalizations related to breathing; 2) Improve lung function; and 3) Improve survival rate. This was a randomized, placebo-controlled trial of warfarin targeting an International Normalized Ratio (INR) of 2.0 to 3.0 in patients with IPF.

The **CENTOCOR TRIAL** is a randomized, placebo-controlled, dose-ranging study to evaluate the efficacy and safety of CNTO 888 given intravenously.

The **ARTEMIS TRIAL** is a randomized and placebo-controlled study to evaluate the efficacy and safety of Ambrisentan in IPF patients. This study will assess whether or not the course of IPF is improved with Ambrisentan.

After nearly five years since my diagnosis with IPF I learned that as the Panther- IPF trial progressed it was discovered that patients had higher mortality rates, hospitalizations, and adverse events with the combination drug compared with the other participants in the study. The trial was stopped for safety, when it became clear that the combination of prednisone and azathioprine was hurting people with idiopathic pulmonary fibrosis (IPF). The data from the Panther Trials is being analyzed to understand why the combination of administered drugs may be detrimental to people with IPF.

I also learned that ACE-IPF trial was stopped early due to increased death with no indication of benefits. This study did not show a benefit for warfarin in the treatment of patients with progressive IPF. Treatment with warfarin increased risk of mortality in an IPF population who lacked other indications for anticoagulation.

From my observations of studies for several years, and personal experience as an engineer, I classify "studies" as either a statistical research study or a basic research study. This may be an oversimplification but statistical research is by nature the recording, organizing, and presenting data ("Trials" fall in this category). On the other hand, basic research studies involve the analysis of all studies, basic science with actual tissues, the use of a microscope and other instrumentation, and also includes studies with animals. I am not sure that any of the results of these studies are made known to the public, but only published in technical journals that are not widely read, even by doctors. Even a primary care doctor does not know what basic research is being done, nor does the doctor have the time to find out! In the case of Pulmonary Fibrosis, I have wondered if they have taken these diseased tissues into the laboratory and experimented by introducing drugs and watching with a microscope the effects; I admit that this is an oversimplification of the disease.

My dad had reasonably good health in his later years. But a couple years before his death, he had some fluid build-up in his lungs. Eventually the doctors told him that they needed to do a biopsy of his lung to verify the problem. So he consented to the surgical procedure. But what he did not know was that the procedure would be done by a couple of resident surgeons. He had a stroke and never regained consciousness, and died in the hospital at the age of 77. Thinking on it now, I often wonder if the doctors purposely kept him sedated. My brother recalls that the results of the biopsy was a finding of pulmonary fibrosis!

I don't understand why the University doing the studies don't follow-up with me and collect data such as my weight, my family history, my diet, etc. Also they could mail up-to-date information to doctors who have patients with certain diseases, ailments, etc. There could be useful information collected from those who do not volunteer for a study! My internal medicine doctor never mentions anything about new research studies, their results, etc.! You would think that because my name is in the University's system that I would receive information relative to trial results, research results, etc. Universities enjoy the research dollars, but don't seem to be focused on the end result, i.e. solving a medical problem, **finding a cure**.

My Mother had reasonably good health during her life, except the last ten years she suffered short-term memory loss. As a result she could not enjoy a movie or a book, and we also learned that she was unable to administer her own medications. She would not remember that she had taken her medications and would over-medicate. This resulted in her becoming agitated and hallucinating. She died at the age of 92.

Let's review why I had neck surgery in 2003. I had taken our grandson skiing on February 1, 2003. As we were driving to the ski resort, we heard on the radio that the spaceship Columbia disintegrated during re-entry resulting in the deaths of all seven crew members aboard because of a faulty heat shield. It was the spaceship's 28th mission. We continued to the ski resort and proceeded to ski. At one point, as I was getting off a ski lift, I ran into some snowboarders who had fallen in front of me. I tried to pick myself up, using my ski poles; however, being on a flat surface, I strained myself.

I continued skiing the rest of the day and everything felt normal. But a week later I started sensing a weakness in my right arm, and I noticed that I could not raise my right arm as high as the day before. I saw an orthopedic doctor and he determined that it could be partial rotator cuff tear, and prescribed physical therapy. After a week or so, the physical therapist thought I should have further tests. A scan indicated stenosis in the neck area that was crowding the nerves. I then saw my neurosurgeon and decided on surgery as soon as possible. The surgery was a two-day surgery: first by placing a plate in front of the neck. After this first day surgery, the surgeon told me that the channels to my arm were OK and not the cause of lost arm motion! But we had to finish the process and two days later they placed rods in the back of my neck. But after this surgery, I was taken to Intensive Care for a few days. After a couple of weeks I was released from the hospital. I went home with a catheter and oxygen, and did not understand why. My surgeon made appointments for me to see a pulmonary specialist, and another neurologist for a nerve conduction tests.

I was never told that one of the two nerves that control my diaphragms for breathing had been severed, most likely during the "closing" phase of the operation. My surgeon had several patients so I suspect he had some resident surgeons close the surgical wound. After the surgery the wound looked terrible and a bone was seen barely under the skin. I suspect that after noting my breathing problems after severing the diaphragm nerves, the surgeons had to rush to close the surgical wound.

After the neck surgery, I started some aggressive physical therapy. A few months later I was back in surgery to put some flesh between skin and bone on back of neck (C7 & C6). After another month or two of physical therapy I was able to have full use of my arm. I have acquired a great respect for physical therapists. But the quote I learned was: "No pain, no gain".

Shortly after my wife and I moved to Utah, we found an attorney to update our Will and other documents. In 2013 I became president of our homeowners association and discovered some serious legal errors in the association's covenants. I then consulted our attorney and we worked together for a few months, revising the covenants and by-laws, and getting them approved and recorded. I shared my story concerning my neck surgery with our attorney and I emailed the following to this attorney: "I don't like the idea of lawsuits, but I abhor dishonesty. In my case, I'm thinking of a minor 'wrist-slapping'". His response was: "We may have a statute of limitations issue. I will research that early next week and follow up". I have never received a response, and I have lost interest.

The surgeon was very skilled and did a good job on my back, and my neck has never caused me any problem. Because of my neck surgery, my physical therapist suggested that I give up skiing. This was hard to do, but I did give up the sport. I now only have memories of our family and friends skiing together. It was great fun. It was also sad because I had bought new "shaped" skis only a year earlier!

I am becoming concerned about an increasing number of political scandals which continue to diminish my faith in our government leadership. The biggest scandal of 2011 was "Fast & Furious", in which the Bureau of Alcohol, Tobacco and Firearms had launched a strategy in 2009, in which it allowed guns to flow into Mexico while the agency tried to identify and charge upper-level cartel members who were buying the guns. However the guns turned up in numerous crimes in Mexico. One of the guns was recovered at the scene where a U.S. Border Patrol Agent was killed.

Among the numerous scandals in 2012 were the White House security leaks of classified information including details of U.S. cyber attacks against Iran; and the Islamic militants attack in Benghazi which killed the U. S. Ambassador and three others, and wounding several others.

There never seems to be any closure in any of these scandals. Top leaders always say they can't discuss anything because they are still "under investigation"!

CHAPTER FOUR

OVERWHELMING NUMBER OF TESTS

MY WIFE HAD CONSIDERED CHANGING her internal medicine doctor after every three-month appointment, explaining that she thought that the doctor didn't like older people. In September of 2013 she had a routine doctor's appointment. A few days later Shirley was notified that blood tests revealed that she was deficient in iron and was given a prescription for iron. The doctor also recommended that she have a colonoscopy; so the doctor scheduled a colonoscopy on 1 October with a gastroenterologist.

The gastroenterologist recommended an esophagogastroduodenoscopy (upper GI endoscopy, i.e. an inspection tube run through the throat to the stomach) in addition to the colonoscopy. After performing both of these procedures, he told me that the colonoscopy revealed colon cancer, and I also <u>think</u> he said that it was Stage 4 because it had gone to the liver (but a colonoscopy could not have revealed this!). He also asked me when I had my last colonoscopy. I told him that it was probably about ten years ago. He said that I should have one. I then checked my records that I had two colonoscopies, one in 1994 and the other in 2001. With my wife's problem and my diagnosis of Pulmonary Fibrosis, I did not want to have a colonoscopy at this time, especially since both previous ones showed no problems, and I had no family history of colon cancer.

The gastroenterologist then scheduled a "Virtual Colonoscopy" for Shirley in the afternoon (same day as the colonoscopy) at a medical facility in Ogden. Air is pumped into the colon and the CT scan is taken. This procedure was very uncomfortable and hurt Shirley. This procedure was performed by a technician with no supervising doctor on site.

The gastroenterologist also scheduled my wife to see a general surgeon the next day in the morning, and a CT scan in the afternoon at the same facility that had done the virtual colonoscopy. The surgeon asked who ordered a virtual colonoscopy and didn't seem to know what it was, or perhaps he was surprised that it was ordered after a colonoscopy. Thus we thought that we should seek a second opinion. We subsequently met with another surgeon and we selected him to do the surgery.

The CT Scan procedure was administered by a technician, and again, no physician was present in the facility. A reaction occurred in my wife's arm where the dye was injected and her arm became swollen. She was instructed to hold her arm above her head for nearly an hour. The technician stated that he would have the doctor look at it. We waited, and about an hour later the technician said that we could leave now; we asked about the doctor looking at her arm. The technician said that her arm was OK and that "the doctor trusts me". We did not notice any images in the radiologist report. There is a question why the CT scan was not scheduled at the local hospital. Perhaps it could not be scheduled on short notice.

The gastroenterologist also scheduled a PET radiation scan five days later. (This test was performed in a specially configured vehicle which visits various facilities on a weekly basis)

These tests were forced on us quickly before we had the time to learn more about these procedures. We were never told the cost of these procedures, probably because we are blessed with good medical insurance coverage. After searching websites on the internet about these tests, I believe that they were not all necessary.

The Mayo Clinic website states that a "**Virtual colonoscopy is an alternative to colonoscopy**... If virtual colonoscopy shows abnormalities in your colon, your doctor will typically recommend colonoscopy to learn more... **Risks include**: tear (perforation) can occur in the colon or rectum wall due to the colon and rectum being inflated with air and radiation exposure may be a concern. However, the level of radiation used during the type of CT scan in virtual colonoscopy is lower than the amount used in a diagnostic CT scan".

I now realized that I am a "caregiver", and many concerns occupied my mind including the need to "scale-down" and get rid of "stuff". But I also realized that it was too late, not the right time when Shirley was being stressed with medical procedures.

At this time I got involved with her medications and organized a weekly procedure to put the medications in pills in a weekly pill boxes, one for morning and another for evening medications. I was starting to get busy with her regular blood tests (Pro Time *), doctor appointments, lab tests, daily care and meals, and anticipated chemo appointments.

 * **A prothrombin time (Pro Time or PT) test measures how quickly your blood clots. The results of this blood test are given as a number that represents a ratio called the International Normalized Ratio (INR).**

CHAPTER FIVE

HOSPITALIZATION AND SURGERY

IN MID-OCTOBER, 2013 MY WIFE had colon surgery at a hospital in Ogden. After the surgery the surgeon told us that he had removed a foot of colon and reconnected it to the small intestine and that he also installed a Power Port (Port-a-cath) in her chest for intravenous connection for chemo treatments. Before the surgery the surgeon told us that most patients could be sent home in three days, but he liked to keep them in the hospital four days. The hospital stay was extended because of nausea and not eating. A feeding tube was inserted for about a week.

After eight days in the hospital, Shirley & I were told about a bacterium in the hospital that they called C. difficile or C. diff. I had been in her room 14-15 hours daily for eight days and no one warned me of this bacteria. I noticed medical staff entering nearby rooms wearing protective clothing and masks but I did not know the reason. My wife was tested for C. diff and it was positive. During this time in the hospital, up to three different antibiotics were administered to her simultaneously.

By searching the websites I discovered that **Clostridium difficile** (C. difficile or C. diff) is a bacterium that can cause symptoms ranging from diarrhea to life-threatening inflammation of the colon. It most commonly affects older adults in hospitals or in long-term care facilities and typically occurs after use of antibiotic medications (especially after the administration of excessive number of antibiotics, simultaneously). C. diff spreads mainly on hands from person to person, and from objects commonly touched. Some people carry the bacterium C. diff in their intestines but never become sick, though they can still spread the infection.

I also learned that on February 8, 2012, the U.S. Food and Drug Administration (FDA) informed the public that **the use of stomach acid drugs known as proton pump inhibitors (PPIs), such as Omeprazole (prilosec) may be associated with an increased risk of C. diff** and recommended that a diagnosis of C. diff be considered for patients taking PPIs who develop diarrhea that does not improve.

I observed that each day there were different medical staff (including nurses and aids), and that they worked 12-hour shifts. The actual time was 13 or 14 hours because of the "turnover" procedures with the new shift. The medical staff works three or four days a week. Some of the hospital staff also have "part-time" jobs at other nursing/rehab facilities or other hospitals.

One nurse was about five months pregnant. She also worked the 12 hour shift routine. She told me that another pregnant nurse worked on the day that she delivered her baby. After the nurse completed her shift, she called her husband and told him that she was going up to the 5th floor to deliver her baby! Indeed, she delivered a full-term healthy baby.

Nurses have immense responsibilities for their patients to administer the proper medications on time; to visit their rooms on a regular basis, to be fully alert and attentive to all of the patients needs. It seems to me that allowing nurses to work long shifts, and also work in the last few months of pregnancy, is a serious risk for the patients, and the hospitals.

Truck drivers and airplane pilots have stringent restrictions as to the number of hours driving or piloting. Why would nurses have little or no restrictions?

After nine days my wife was released from hospital and transferred to a Nursing & Rehab facility near our home. She suffered from pain and nausea during this time, and continued to have diarrhea. I believe that the virtual colonoscopy procedure, performed on the same day as a colonoscopy, hurt my wife and was the cause for her extended stay in the hospital.

CHAPTER SIX

FIRST EXPERIENCE AT A NURSING FACILITY

WHILE CHECKING INTO THE NURSING facility we first met her nurse. When she came to my wife's room to remove the dinner tray, she asked my wife if she had completed her dinner. My wife responded that she wanted to keep her bread. Then the nurse picked up the bread with her bare hands and set it aside. I did not say anything, but it left me an impression.

The next day, the same nurse dropped off a small cup of many pills. I asked her what they were and she promptly poured the pills into her bare hand and started to explain what the pills were! I questioned her on this and she responded that her hands were clean. But I wondered how many other patients' pills were taken into her hand? I talked to the head of nursing about this at the time.

One evening my son & I were in my wife's room. The same nurse gave my wife a pill for "insomnia" so that my wife would sleep better. I asked the name of the drug and she wrote it out as "**seroquel**". **She said that it was a spare drug in her drawer that she can give patients if the prescribed medications don't seem to work!** I then learned that she had been giving the drug to Shirley for at least two days. I told her that seroquel was not on the approved list of drugs for **my wife**. Then her story changed.

In checking websites about the drug **seroquel**, I found that it is used to treat bipolar disorder and has some very serious side effects, **death being listed near the top of the list.** One website posted: "**... Antidepressants have increased the risk of suicidal thoughts ... Patients of all ages starting treatment should be watched closely for worsening of depression, suicidal thoughts or actions, unusual changes in behavior, agitation, and irritability. ...Stroke that can lead to death can happen in elderly people ...**"

My wife experienced a set back in her wellness program for two days, including becoming irritable, confused, weak, dizzy, etc. ----- all side effects attributed to this drug.

My wife's internal medicine doctor had just adjusted her medicine that gave her a drug to help her sleep. The nurse claimed that she got the doctor's permission (a changed story) for seroquel and had called a doctor who was standing in for my wife's doctor. Not true. The nurse finally said that she got a staff doctor to OK it, probably not even reviewing Shirley's medical condition. If a staff doctor approved it, it was after the fact, that is, after she had already given my wife the pill two or three times.

When I left the nursing home the previous night, I did **not** note that **seroquel** had been recorded as being given to my wife, but my son & I watched as she took the medicine given her. The nurse said that the dosage was two 25mg pills. **Where did she get this medication?**

I hand-delivered a letter to the manager of the Nursing/Rehab facility. The letter addressed several concerns: 1) The nurses should not change a drug order without an advanced order from a doctor who is familiar with the patient; 2) The drug-administering nurse should observe that the patient takes the prescribed drugs, then promptly record the information -- medicine, time, dosage; 3) The nurses should have knowledge of the drugs which they are administering; 4) Drugs should be administered in a timely manner. For example, one of my wife's drugs was to be given three times a day; one four times a day. They need to be spread out and not missed; 5) Nurses need to follow cleanliness guidelines; and 6) Nurses should not work longer than 12 hours within a 24 hours period. My wife's nurse had worked many more hours than a 12 hour shift -- more like 15 or 16 hours each day. The nurse told us that she worked a double-shift because another nurse could not work her regular shift! She said that she did not go home and that she worked until 3:00 am, and then slept in a spare bed until about 6:00 am and then continued to work until about 9:00 pm. During her sleep time, who was looking after the patients?

I noted that no doctor had seen Shirley since she arrived at the nursing home despite a noticeable decline in her health. I wonder how left-over medicines are disposed for patients who are released from the hospital, nursing or rehab facilities. Do nurses keep their own stockpile of drugs, like Seroquel? I never received a response to my letter from the Nursing home.

CHAPTER SEVEN

HOSPITAL AGAIN AND START OF CHEMO

AFTER ABOUT A WEEK IN the nursing facility our son & I thought Shirley needed medical attention, thus we took her to the Emergency Room of the local hospital. An imaging scan revealed a stomach blockage and she was admitted to the hospital. Her stomach was pumped and diarrhea continued.

Four days later a second esophagogastroduodenoscopy (upper GI endoscopy) was performed while in the hospital. Significant difference in images from the one done at the time of her colonoscopy. Our doctors did not explain or comment on these changes, nor did they tell us why this procedure was done. This seems to be further evidence that the esophagogastroduodenoscopy and/or the Virtual Colonoscopy did some damage.

This virtual colonoscopy hurt my wife and I believe that the procedure upset her system, including nausea and stomach blockages and was the cause for her extended stay in hospital. Doing this procedure on the same day as the regular colonoscopy must have caused additional stress to her system

After five days in the hospital, Shirley was released from hospital and went home. Now I was a "caregiver". I never realized how intense "caregiving" could be until I was faced with these responsibilities. When a member of a family needs help during a medical condition, the caregiver may have to assist in any one of the "daily activities of living" such as bathing, dressing, eating, toileting and transferring (moving the patient within the home & taking to medical facilities as required). In addition, there are other responsibilities including ensuring medications are taken properly and renewed as required, and preparing meals. Then there are the normal "chores" such as laundry, grocery-shopping, washing the dishes, house-cleaning, maintaining the automobiles, paying the bills, yard work, etc.

Chemotherapy was scheduled to be six treatments, two weeks apart. The procedure was to start on a Monday with infusion of chemo drugs for about three hours, then go home for two days with a portable pack which continued to pump chemo drugs into her system. Her first session of chemo was started on 11 November. Shirley's sister Barbara & I took her to the oncologist's facility and wheeled her into a large room with a dozen or more other patients. Before they could start chemo, they drew blood through her 'port" in addition to working for an hour to unclog the port-a-cath. The chemo drugs used were 5-FU, Eloxatin, and Leucovorin calcium. Shirley was weak starting this session of chemo. Late in the day the result of her blood test revealed that she should have a blood transfusion. It seems to me that the blood results also indicated that she should not have started chemo. In a meeting with the oncologist before treatments, he had told us about the drugs he intended to use. One was avastin. After her first treatment I asked him why he had not used avastin. His reply was that her scheduled chemo was too close to her surgery. In other words, there had not been enough time between the surgery and the start of chemo treatments.

Two days later, on a Wednesday, Shirley was weak and we needed two neighbors to help get her in the car. Shirley's sister & I took her to the local Regional Hospital where she had a blood transfusion (two units). In the afternoon, the chemo pump was removed. Cymbalta (Duloxetin), 60 mg was prescribed about this time, not sure why.

The 2nd session of chemo was started two weeks later, on 25 November. She was very weak and again needed to be wheeled into the oncologist's facility. Again after unclogging the Power Port and drawing a blood sample chemo drugs were administered. The blood sample was not analyzed until late in the day at the hospital.

At this time I was spending more time attending to Shirley's needs. We have been blessed with support from family and friends.

Every Thursday I put her morning and evening pills for the next week in the appropriate pill containers; then twice a day I put the pills in a paper cup for her to take. I do four loads of laundry every week, usually two on Wednesday and two on Saturday that includes the bedding. Sometimes it is necessary for another load or two. Unfortunately I never learned a lot of cooking skills. But thanks to microwaves and prepared foods, it is much easier to prepare a meal by persons with little or no cooking skills.

More political scandals occupied my mind in 2013 including (1) The National Security Agency (NSA) was found to have massive data collection programs, snooping on U.S. organizations, American allies, and persons; (2) the IRS improperly targeted Tea Party and other conservative groups and key persons refused to testify during a Congressional hearing; (3) technical problems with the launch of government's website for the "Affordable Care Act" and the President using executive orders to change the legislation; and (4) the Department of Justice (DOJ) snooped on the telephone records of reporters.

As a veteran, I am particularly interested in maintaining our freedoms for future generations.

CHAPTER EIGHT

HOSPITAL A THIRD TIME AND REHAB AGAIN

TWO DAYS LATER, ON A Wednesday, 27 November, I took Shirley to the oncologist's facility to remove the portable chemo pump. Shirley was very weak and found to be dehydrated. She sat for a couple of hours with an IV before the pump was removed. Our son arrived and we proceeded to our car, again in a wheel chair. When we got into the car Shirley was observed to be incoherent and extremely weak; we then took her immediately to the hospital where she was admitted to hospital's Intensive Care Unit (ICU) for three days, then to a regular room. Her pulse rate was erratic and she did not know where she was for three days. We "celebrated" Thanksgiving in the hospital!

On December 7ᵗʰ an x-ray of Shirley's stomach was taken in her room prior to being released from hospital. We have not seen radiologist report of this x-ray. She was then transferred to a different Nursing & Rehab; her white blood cell count was below normal. On December 31ˢᵗ a stool sample was taken to check on the presence of C. diff. A few days later we were told that the test was negative.

I had noticed that her list of medications kept getting longer. The doctor never seemed to review the need to continue some of the medications. Then we discovered several errors in the communications between the doctor's office and the pharmacy. For example, the prescription for Metformin read: "Take two tablets twice daily", meaning take two tablets in the morning and two in the evening. However, the correct prescription should have read "Take one tablet twice daily" meaning take one tablet in the morning and one in the evening". After noting that her blood sugar was well controlled we questioned the dosage and made the correction. Another example of an error was the refilling of a 50 mg prescription. When we got home from the pharmacy we luckily noted that the pills were 100mg ones and the notation was "Take half pill daily". For a prescription of 90 pills, this was unsatisfactory. If we had not noted this change for a refill, my wife would have taken a double dose which would have resulted in another serious medical problem.

During her stay at the Nursing/Rehab facility, we celebrated our anniversary, my birthday, Christmas, and New Years! I began thinking of my own health and hoping that I would continue to be healthy enough to care for my wife. I again wondered whether my pulmonary fibrosis diagnoses was correct, and if so, how much longer would I live.

During the first week in January, 2014, Shirley was released from Rehab and went home. She then sought a second opinion at a cancer facility in Salt Lake City. She wanted to know whether she should resume Chemo, or see if there are other optional treatments available in her case. The doctors were told that Shirley was very weak when she started Chemo, and that she had two sessions of chemo in November, 2013. Shirley got no answers. The doctors wanted her to be a participant in one of the University studies! She was not interested and was very disappointed.

CHAPTER NINE

———— ⤳ ⤶ ————

RE-START OF CHEMO & HOSPITALIZATION

AFTER A DAY OR TWO at home we got a call from the office of Shirley's gastroenterologist. The doctor wanted to schedule her for a third esophagogastroduodenoscopy (upper GI endoscopy). We were never satisfied with all of the tests and procedures that this doctor had ordered, especially the virtual colonoscopy, and we supposed that the insurance "window of allowable charges" was the reason for the procedure, not a medical need. We considered all those tests as not necessary and caused stress on Shirley's digestive system. Thus we did not schedule an additional GI endoscopy. If Shirley had been in the hospital the request would have been made to her internal medicine doctor and the procedure would have been done, whether needed or not! That is the risk one takes when they are in the hospital, especially with good insurance.

Within the next few days we obtained a new gastroenterologist. We had only one visit with the new doctor and we were pleased; he recommended an over-the-counter medicine that was very effective in controlling her diarrhea.

Shirley was scheduled to re-start Chemo infusion soon but the Power Port was plugged. The next day the local Hospital lab tried to unplug the power port with no success.

The surgeon (the one who was originally scheduled to do Shirley's colon surgery) did not want to replace the Power Port (Port-a-cath) at this time; thus on March 11th the hospital Infusion Lab installed a "Pick" line in her right arm; later in the day she **re-started Chemo**, but finished Chemo on the following day.

The "new" Chemo was scheduled weekly for six weeks, with two weeks off before starting another six weeks of chemo. Each chemo session lasted about three hours. During this six-week interval, the surgeon removed the Power Port in his office.

At the conclusion of each chemo session, I had to take Shirley to the hospital infusion lab to have her pick line cleaned with a new bandage as we were told that this pick-line could be a source of serious infection. The pick-line also presented additional care in preparation for showers -- a rubber sleeve had to be put on her arm in order to prevent water from getting to the bandage. Thus we concluded that a pick line is high maintenance, and extra trips to the hospital infusion lab.

Shirley completed the last of the six weeks of chemo and had experienced no side effects or problems; however, two days after the sixth treatment, she suddenly lost her appetite and was noticeably weaker. After another day or two I became concerned and drove Shirley to Hospital ER. She was tested and released.

Three days later, I drove her again to Hospital ER. This time she was admitted to the hospital and was taken to the ICU (Intensive Care Unit), and started an IV with food content. A few days later they removed her catheter and other tubes, and moved her to a regular hospital room.

I was trying to analyze why after six weeks of treatment she suddenly became weak. Could it be an accumulative effect of the chemo drugs, or was the drug given on the sixth week significantly stronger than the previous weekly doses?

During this time, I changed my internal medicine doctor. I had the same doctor as my wife, but I lost trust in the doctor. With my responsibilities as a "caregiver" for my wife, I could not afford any problems with this doctor. We tried to change her doctor too, but all the doctors in her clinic would not accept her because of agreements between the doctors. Seeking a doctor in another facility, like I did, would present additional problems relative to convenience of other services close to home, like checking her blood Pro Time every week or two, so we decided to keep the doctor but be alert, knowing that when one is in the hospital, you lose control -- the doctor controls everything: IVs, medications, procedures (e.g. X-rays, esophagogastroduodenoscopy); we were never sure what the medical staff was doing. Also the oncologist mixes the chemo medications so one never knows for sure the contents of the doses.

Along with providing care for Shirley, or monitoring her progress I became more agitated with the political environment, and feeling that the citizens of this great country are in jeopardy of losing our health, safety, and freedoms. The suggestion that African ebola patients will be treated in this country is frightening. How will U.S. citizens be protected? Then there is the question of the proper quarantine period for ebola and the general question of immigrating persons with diseases.

CHAPTER TEN

REHAB A THIRD TIME AND HOME

IN EARLY MAY HER "PICK" was removed from Shirley's arm and she was released from the hospital the next day and transferred to a rehabilitation ("rehab") facility. This was her third time in a nursing/rehab facility and the second time in this one. She liked this rehab facility and the staff was very efficient and helpful.

After a week in Rehab, Shirley started to show improvement with greater strength. The physical and occupational therapists worked with her every day and she continually showed improvement. I bought a meal ticket and ate lunch and dinner with her and a few other patients. During her stay in Rehab I took her to appointments for her eye doctor and hairdresser. She had to use a walker, but we managed OK.

After nearly a month in Rehab, Shirley was finally released to go home. On this same day we drove to Idaho Falls to celebrate an 80th birthday reception for a friend. This event allowed us to visit with many other friends and was very good for Shirley after all of the problems that she had faced for the previous seven and a half months. A week after this trip to Idaho, we traveled several hundred miles to attend the funeral of her brother who died of cancer. She did very well traveling and we stopped frequently along the way. Then, three months later, we drove to Bellingham, WA to visit Shirley's older sister. The traveling went well and Shirley helped with the driving!

Shirley has been home now for nine months. She looks good, has a great appetite, and can walk freely without even using a cane. After the first month home, Shirley was strong enough to re-start our morning water aerobics class every day. We are able to go anywhere, and it has made life easier for both of us. I still help her with her medications, do the laundry, and prepare meals if we are not able to dine out. We are constantly busy with doctor appointments, hair appointments, and checking her Pro Time. We were also able to attend many entertainment programs during the summer months. The fact that we can dine out and attend programs is a real relief from the previous seven months.

Shirley has been blessed. Her body was able to respond to emergency treatments, and those attending her were able to make the right decisions. The attending doctors and nurses at the emergency room of the hospital got her started on appropriate procedures and medications; her family monitored her health very closely and took action when necessary. I have also been blessed in as much as my health has been stable and I'm able to take care of Shirley.

Now it has been nearly five years since my diagnosis of pulmonary fibrosis (PF). I feel fine, but short of breath at times, probably due to partial loss of lung diaphragm function. Two years ago I had a cough for about a week; I went to our "Instant-care" facility and treated with an anti-biotic and a mouth spray and have had no other problems since then.

I again wonder about the PF diagnosis. Is the fibrosis slow-growing at this time? Why doesn't my doctor say anything about my disease when I see him for a routine visit? I am grateful that I feel as though there is nothing wrong with me. We only revealed the diagnosis of PDF to our immediate family, my brothers, and my former doctor in Idaho.

Political scandals continued in 2014: (1) the unsatisfactory treatment of veteran patients by the Department of Veterans Affairs in which dozens died while waiting for care; and (2) an intruder climbed a White House fence, entered the White House through an unlocked door, evading several agents.

Many friends suggest remedies for cancer including diet items, medications, etc. It is sometimes frustrating to believe all of the conflicting information when trying to confirm on various websites. None of the suggested remedies seemed to be a cure, but rather for prevention.

CHAPTER ELEVEN

OTHER TREATMENT OPTIONS

IN LATE SEPTEMBER, 2014, WE had an appointment with Shirley's oncologist to discuss optional treatments: 1) a weekly dose of erbitux, injected for an hour, or 2) a daily pill stivarga. The doctor said that he would check to see if the specialty drug would be covered by our insurance.

A few days later we received a surprise call from our mail-order pharmacy that they were ready to deliver the drug, starvarga, but wanted us to know that we had not met all of our annual deductible which was over $1,000. For specialty drugs the mail-order pharmacy is the only one that can provide it. We told the drug company not to deliver, that we had not decided on a treatment. We asked the pharmacy the retail cost of the drug. We were told the cost is $23,000 for 84 pills!

Information about these drugs:

> **Erbitux (Cetuximab)** - The most common side effects are rash, itching, nail changes, headache, diarrhea, and respiratory, skin, and mouth infections. Other side effects are nausea, vomiting, constipation, stomachache, backache, fever/chills, trouble sleeping, weight loss, fatigue, drowsiness, eye redness/itching, dry skin, and mouth/throat sores may occur. Nausea and vomiting can be quite severe.

Stivarga (Regorafenib) - Stivarga is a "specialty" drug" prescription used to treat colon or rectal cancer that has spread to other parts of the body and for which the patient had received previous treatment with certain chemotherapy medicines. It is also used to treat other types of cancers.

*The manufacturer warns: "****Stivarga can cause liver problems,*** *which can be serious and sometimes lead to death. Your healthcare provider will do blood tests to check your liver function before you start taking Stivarga and during your treatment with Stivarga to check for liver problems".*

STIVARGA may cause serious side effects, including: 1) severe bleeding which can be serious and **sometimes lead to death**; 2) a skin problem called hand-foot skin reaction and severe skin rash; 3) high blood pressure; 4) a condition called reversible posterior leukoencephalopathy syndrome (RPLS); 5) a tear in your stomach or intestinal wall (bowel perforation) that can be serious and sometimes lead to death; and 6) wound healing problems. Other problems include tiredness, weakness, fatigue, diarrhea, loss of appetite, swelling, pain, and redness of the lining in your mouth, throat, stomach, bowel (mucositis), voice changes or hoarseness, infection, pain in other parts of your body, weight loss, and nausea. Ref: www.stivarga-us.com/index.html.

The oncologist had told us that studies have shown that life expectancy was increased by only two months with the pill, compared with those with no treatment. Clearly the benefit does not outweigh the risks or cost. The doctor could not give us any information regarding Shirley's life expectancy or what symptoms she might experience if the cancer were spreading or affecting her life.

A week later, in late October, 2014, Shirley & I met again with the oncologist. Shirley expressed that she would like to do something. The doctor again discussed options: 1) weekly injections of **Erbitux** or 2) a daily pill, **Stivarga**. The doctor stated some of the side effects of each option. Shirley said she would like to start with Erbitux, and scheduled the weekly infusion to start the following week. They would have to find a vein every week -- not good.

A few days later, she decided not to have the treatments and called the doctor's office to cancel.

The following day, her oncologist called and said that the side effects might not be bad at all! He suggested the pill might be the better alternative. Then Shirley asked him if a "milder" form of the chemo treatments that were given in March and April would work. The doctor acknowledged that it may work, but Shirley said that she would want to have another "Power Port" implanted in her chest, which is an operating room procedure at the hospital. Shirley told the doctor that she would re-think all of the options.

Shirley's oncologist did not mention any preliminary blood tests or on-going blood tests for Stivarga! And his staff told Shirley that we would not have to pay the rest of our deductible! One has to wonder what gratuities doctors receive from drug companies for prescribing their drugs!

This seems to be unbelievable: no blood tests, deductible covered by doctor's office, and the doctor's call after Shirley had told his staff to cancel the Erbitux treatments. The push was clearly for the pill. Recalling the start of Chemo in November, 2013, Shirley was very weak and the blood tests just prior to starting Chemo did not support the decisions to start Chemo, and the oncologist used different chemo drugs than what he had planned to use.

Shirley felt that she should be receiving some treatment in order to extend her life. I think doing nothing is better than any options that we have heard so far. She had a CT scan in early August and as I recall there was very little comment other than a little change. Additional CT scans or tests were not suggested by Shirley's doctor, nor were other types of treatments such as radiation. I can only provide information for my wife that I get from websites; Shirley has to make any decision for future treatments. The doctors cannot, or will not, disclose an estimate of life expectancy. The gastroenterologist who performed the colonoscopy gave a distinct impression that life expectancy was very short, citing Stage IV; and her oncologist initially indicated that it was short, but recently has not made any predictions. If this information were known then one could evaluate treatment options relative to benefits vs. risks/ misery. If a treatment option would extend life a few months or a year or more, the decision would be easier.

Shirley still wonders if she should have additional treatments. She wonders if the chemo treatments were helpful in extending her life. I'm not sure. The treatments landed her in the hospital each time it was started, and the side effects were devastating but she was able to overcome them with time. Shirley has made another appointment with her oncologist in early December. She has not received any treatments (Chemo) for seven and half months.

In the early hours of 18 Nov. 2014 Shirley felt pain on her right side. Just before noon she said that she needed to see a doctor. The doctor's office told us to go to the hospital ER. We arrived there shortly after noon and did not leave until 6:00 pm. They did various blood tests and a CT Scan. The doctors commented on the CT scan: noted a narrowing where her colon surgery was performed. Other tests revealed a urinary infection and provided a prescription for Nitrofurantoin Mono/Mac100 mg caps; two each day for five days.

While these medical options were being discussed and evaluated, I was worried about the many political issues in our country, the most glaring one was the issue of mail-in ballots. By State law, we learned that the various County Clerks can decide the method of voting. Our County Clerk changed the voting method from a poll booth to Mail-in ballots only. This raises a lot of concerns: who is actually voting, secrecy of the ballot, ballot counting and validation procedures, mail fraud, receipt of ballots, etc. I spent a lot of time writing letters and emails, but to no avail.

Shirley saw her oncologist in early December. He discussed alternative treatments. A blood sample was taken to check a particular marker. Four days later we got the results of blood test via phone call with her oncologist. Shirley decided on Erbitux treatment but did not want to start until after the holidays.

Shirley saw her eye doctor about ten days later and her eye was injected with Eylea, a treatment for wet macular degeneration.

In late December we delivered a letter to her primary care doctor requesting a referral for an oncologist for a second opinion relative to any future cancer treatments. The doctor's office said that her doctor would be out of the office for a week and that the doctors who are filling-In for him could not make a referral.

Two days later Shirley decided that she would change her primary care doctor. She had been contemplating this for several months. She kept thinking of the times the doctor told her: *"If anything should happen to you, we would have to decide whether to treat it or not"*. That is not what she wanted to hear. Again, she chose to use the same doctor that I had. We learned that this presented a problem when checking her Pro Time (INR). The doctor's office did not have a portable reader for this purpose; instead she had to have her blood withdrawn and tested. This was especially hard for Shirley since finding her veins was not an easy matter, and she was "poked" two or three times each time they checked her INR.

In early January 2015, we met with an oncologist in Ogden for a second opinion. A few days later we met with a surgeon to schedule installing a new port in Shirley's chest. This procedure was scheduled and after some time in the operating room, the surgeon reported that he was unable to install the port! Shirley was subsequently scheduled to have the hospital specialty personnel install the port the next day.

Nearly three weeks later Shirley started the Infusion of Erbitux at the oncologist office in Ogden. This treatment was scheduled every week on Tuesday.

There was a problem in adjusting her blood-thinning medication, warfarin. Her diet has remained constant, yet since she started treatments with Erbitux, her INR has been up and down – as high as 10.3 and low as 1.1. Ideally the doctors want to keep the INR between 2 & 3.

When it was 10.3 she had to have two units of blood plasma to bring it down. And now after seven week of treatments, her INR is still increasing, and she had to have another unit of blood plasma.

We did manage to visit Idaho Falls for two nights, 9 & 10 April to visit friends. We had breakfast with teachers, principal and staff from the school where Shirley taught (spouses were also invited!). We also had a dinner with another group of friends. On the second day we enjoyed a dinner with our former travel group. These social events really thrilled Shirley and seemed to give her greater strength.

On 15 April I had an appointment with my primary care doctor (internal medicine). The doctor informed me that he and two other doctors were leaving the corporation! This is also Shirley's doctor; thus a search begins for new doctors.

Shirley's INR keeps changing and it is noted that the treatments are acting as a blood thinner. Her warfarin medication for thinning the blood has gone from 22.5 mg per week before treatments to lower doses: 15 mg per week, then 5 mg per week, and then to no medication.

On Saturday, 18 April 2015 – Shirley's appetite was low and did not eat much. Her foot was more swollen than usual. On Sunday her diet was practically nothing. Her foot was still very swollen so I started to wonder if her furosemide medication (a diuretic, i.e. water tablets) was the correct one. I had refilled this prescription on 3 April and the shape of the pill was different, a very small white round pill as opposed to the earlier pill which was in a very small football-shaped pill. I had learned that a change in a color or shape of a pill is common because different pharmaceutical companies make the same pill to the same specification. But in this case I wanted to make sure.

Thus I went to the pharmacy and I was shown that the prescription was properly filled. I described the symptoms (loss of appetite, swollen feet) and I was told that this could be a very dangerous situation and might mean kidney failure or heart attack.

I then took Shirley to a local "instant-care" facility to see a doctor. They tested her blood and I was told that her potassium level was critically high. I was told to take her to the hospital emergency desk and check her in as an out-patient and have her blood tested again for potassium level. They did all sorts of tests (EKG, etc.) and started to connect her for an IV before any doctor orders. We were at the hospital from late afternoon until 10:00 pm! They wanted to draw blood a third time and we protested because Shirley's arm was getting bruised all over from the attempts to get her blood. We asked why for a third time, and were told that they wanted to see the "trend". We soon got the feeling that all of this was to increase corporate profits rather than for the "benefit" of the patient.

I finally got the report of her Potassium (K) level (5.6 mmol/L) where the normal range is 3.6 – 5.1). Then I noticed that her weekly treatments at her oncologist's office that her potassium level was also at that level a week or so earlier! We were told not to give her the daily potassium pill. Her potassium was 5.2 on 24 April, and Shirley seems to be getting weaker and sleeps more.

In the early morning (3:00 am) on 30 April (Thursday) Shirley woke me and said that she had shortness of breath and was concerned about the swelling in her legs and ankles. We decided to go to the living room because she said that she could breath easier in her recliner than in bed. About a half hour later she said that she should go to the ER at the hospital. We got to the hospital about 4:00am. They did some blood tests and an Xray. The ER doctor said that there is indication of water in the lung. He talked with Shirley's new "primary care" doctor and described his findings. We were at the hospital until about 6:00 am. We then learned that his office was closed on Thursdays.

The next day, Friday, we called Shirley's new primary care doctor's office and managed to get an appointment at 10:15 am. The doctor called in a prescription for an anti-biotic (5 days) for pneumonia. He scheduled a CT scan later this day (1:50 pm). He scheduled for a procedure to withdraw fluid from the lung and also check the material for cancer – procedure scheduled for Thursday, 7 May 2015. But because Shirley's blood INR was greater than 1.5, the procedure was re-scheduled for Friday, 8 May. Her INR was 1.4 on Thursday so Shirley met the requirements.

The radiologist withdrew a lot of fluid from her right lung area and sent it to lab for analysis. She then had a chest X-ray to ensure that the lung was not punctured. Then her primary care doctor had her go to the lab for blood tests.

The results of the analysis of the lung fluid indicated no cancer.

Shirley's blood Pro Time continued to be erratic: on Friday, 22 May her INR was 2.2 and on Friday, 29 May the INR was 11.1! Her doctor prescribed that she take two Mephyton 5mg tablets and have her blood pro- time tested the next day. The next day her INR was 1.2 and the following two days it was 2.5 and 3.9.

We met with Shirley's oncologist. He wants her to be part of a study: A Randomized, Double-Blind Study of Ruxolitinib or Placebo in Combination With Regorafenib (Stivarga) in Subjects With Relapsed or Refractory Metastatic Colorectal Cancer (Study No. INCB 18424-287, Sponsor: Incyte Corporation).

On 3 June 2015 Shirley's new primary care doctor prescribed another "water tablet", Metolazone 5mg. As a result the swelling in her legs and ankles has gone down a little.

Five days later Shirley decided to discontinue any further cancer treatments and not be a part of the study. The drug, Stivarga (Regorafenib) was shown to extend life only two months, and it was particular hard on the liver and could cause serious bleeding. Taking this drug alone was an option that Shirley considered earlier. But taking it with another drug with unknown consequences, the constant testing, etc. just seemed to be too much. She had been taking Erbitux treatments weekly for over four months. The driving to Ogden was another risk for older drivers like myself, but I was willing to do it if Shrley wanted additional treatments. The good thing we learned about the study was the fact that one of the requirements for being included in the study was a life expectancy of 12 weeks or more! Her oncologist never said anything about life expectancy.

On Wednesday morning, 17 June 2015 Shirley asked me to take her to the hospital. She felt that she was dying. About 10:45 I took her to the hospital, ER. After a long day of tests, at about 5:45 pm, the doctor, without saying anything about the results of tests, etc., asked us if we had considered hospices! I was expecting her be admitted to the hospital. After talking to some hospital staff people, we decided to admit her to a local Home Health & Hospice.

A van from the facility came and took her there and I went home briefly to get some items for Shirley, etc. When I arrived at the facility she was in a room where the air conditioner was not working and they had no plan to fix it. Our son also noted that the adjoining room also had a faulty air conditioning unit. We complained and then moved Shirley to a much better room in a wing that they had said was either full or that they could not take hospice patients!

On Thursday morning I went to the Hospice facility and saw that Shirley's eyes were closed and did not respond. She was breathing heavily. The nurse said that she was given a nausea pill about 3:00 a.m. I left the room to sign papers for her admittance, etc. and when I returned to the room she was not breathing. The nurse looked at her and said that she had passed away --- time given was 9:30 a.m. However the death certificate states that she died at 10:05 a.m. That was about the time that they notified the mortuary.

CHAPTER TWELVE

※ ※

SENIORS IN A CHANGING WORLD

I HAVE OBSERVED FOR SEVERAL years that many retired senior citizens work at the polls during election time. They are usually people you know or recognize. Many seniors also communicate with their friends and relatives regarding various political issues, and get upset when they see traditional values and culture changing. There are concerns that these changes will affect our republic and our grandchildren in the future.

In March, 2012 Shirley & I attended a Republican caucus meeting at a school close to our home. Since we were relatively new residents of Utah we were eager to find out how the political processes work in Utah. I have always been interested in current issues and I write or forward many emails to friends, write letters to newspaper editors, and write letters to my representatives in the U.S. Congress as well as State legislators. When we attended this caucus meeting I brought some handouts as to how I felt about current issues and candidates. One of the agenda items of the caucus meeting was to elect officers of the caucus as well as State Delegates for the upcoming convention. I was nominated for State Delegate and then elected! Shirley was also elected as Vice Chairman of the Caucus. This was the first time that we had ever been active in the political process other than studying the issues and candidates, then voting.

I subsequently attended the State GOP Convention in Sandy, Utah (Salt Lake City area) in April 2012. This was a great experience. I heard an outstanding speech by Mia Love who was running for U.S. Congress. She received a standing ovation, but was defeated in the election that year. But in 2014, she was elected the first black female Republican as well as first Haitian American in the U.S. Congress. She is also the first black person to be elected to Congress from Utah.

As a result of being elected a Republican State Delegate, I receive daily phone calls, emails, and U.S. mail requesting donations for support of various political action groups or campaigns. Apparently my telephone number, email address, and physical address were disseminated to many organizations. **I find that raising political funds is a year-round activity! Out-of-state money is influencing local elections!**

The country is in distress and I spend a lot of time addressing various issues in one form or another. The responses from members of Congress, obviously written by a staff member or an intern seldom address the issues presented; thus the member of Congress most likely never read or been adequately briefed of constituent concerns.

For elderly seniors like myself, it is frustrating to see the changes around us. I am concerned about all of the political scandals, social issues (same-sex marriage, transgender restrooms, etc.), TV advertising of sexual products, defacing of the human body with tattoos, denigration of religion, massive unlawful immigration, lack of national security, political leaders who demonstrate that they know nothing about protection of classified material, massive national debt with no effort for solving, lack of controls for campaign financing, the increased prospect of fraudulent ballots because of mail-in ballots, non-transparent government, dishonest members of congress, and the non-enforcement of federal laws (e.g. drugs and borders). A search on the web shows that about a hundred former members of Congress have been indicted or imprisoned in the last twenty years!

I believe that enforcing drug laws is critical for many reasons, one of which is national security. If our young men and women are hooked on drugs, there will not be enough qualified personnel to defend this country; they will not be capable of operating the sophisticated weapons in today's military arsenal.

I wish I could be optimistic about the political future for America. It seems like the younger generation is moving towards socialism at an alarming rate, and most of these younger people do not understand what that will mean, and they vote! The use of "executive orders" by a President in order to bypass Congress is one sign of an emerging dictatorship associated with socialism. Other signs of emerging dictatorship are gun control and using federal agencies to spy on Congress and citizens. Meanwhile Congress does nothing except increasing the national debt for re-election purposes.

The number of political scandals is growing, one being the non-protection of classified information by legislators, cabinet officers, and appointees. Security leaks abound from government sources, including the White House staff, legislators, cabinet officers and other appointees. The so-called security of U.S. classified materials seems to be an easy target for hackers and foreign agents. Government agencies (CIA and FBI) should be actively analyzing the security of various communication sources to see if they can be hacked or otherwise vulnerable to foreign intelligence organizations. Any violations should then prompt action to correct the deficiencies.

Persons who have access to classified information should be able to recognize what is "sensitive information", and also know that even their personal mail can reveal information that is classified. Any official who originates a message needs to classify it, and be intelligent enough to do so. Certainly any correspondence of any type between the White House and the Secretary of State certainly should have a security classification, in fact most all communications with a Secretary of State would most likely be classified confidential, secret, or top secret.

In 2009, after noting the backgrounds of the White House staff, I wrote a letter to one of my U. S. Senators about my concern for granting security clearances to White House staff. Several weeks went by and I got a response which included a letter from the Federal Bureau of Investigation (FBI), quoted in part as follows:

> "The Federal Bureau of Investigation (FBI) conducts background investigations (BI) on behalf of the White House. The BIs involve interviews and records checks. The sole purpose of BIs is fact-gathering and no suitability or security decisions are made by the FBI.

> "The FBI has no knowledge of the clearance requirements for White House employees or Presidential appointees. The White House staff are granted clearances through the Office of Security and Emergency Preparedness, Executive Office of the President. Clearances for Presidential appointees which require Senate confirmation are adjudicated and issued through the agency to which they are being appointed."

The Senator should have had concerns, but did not. He took no action. In 2012 there were White House security leaks. An investigation was promised, and I have heard no results. Then in 2015 we learned about classified information transmitted as though the material was unclassified with an unauthorized server.

The foregoing procedures by the FBI should be reviewed and revised. Just looking at some of the personnel working in the White House and knowing some of their backgrounds, they would never get a security clearance during the time I was serving in the military.

The, Senate Homeland Security & Government Affairs Committee and the Senate Select Committee on Intelligence have responsibilities to train the legislatures, White House staff, and appointees concerning security matters such as the classifications, need to know criteria, how to handle classified information, safeguards, etc. The poor performance of these committees is evident with the on-going email and server scandal. Also the CIA and FBI should continually be monitoring transmissions of government correspondence for any evidence of being unsecure. Very few members of Congress are commenting on various probes of possible violations of national security laws! Could it be that all of them are sloppy or ignorant with national security requirements?

My military service taught me four basic classifications of correspondence in the military: Unclassified, Confidential, Secret, and Top Secret. Every piece of correspondence (letters or messages) noted the classification. Any classification other than unclassified was handled with the utmost strict procedures. **I also learned that there are at least three elements to the security of classified information: 1) proper level of clearance based on background investigation, 2) need to know (a structured approach to limiting access), and 3) training on how to handle classified information.** It is important to enforce "need to know" criteria.

Couple these political and social problems with the responsibilities of a caregiver and various medical problems, my mind is constantly in a "whirlwind". When I was not attending to my wife's needs I was spending time at my computer writing this book, looking up medical information on the internet, and forwarding or composing emails.

I was also sending emails or letters to members of the U.S. Congress and State legislators, a few to national VIPs, and governors. These writings and political analysis helped me deal with the political stresses; it provided a feeling of finding potential solutions to conflicts.

Another major problem is the negotiations with Iran relative to their nuclear program that threatens the world. It has been 70 years since the atom bomb was used to end WWII. When the Middle East countries get a nuclear weapon they will not hesitate to use it; there will be no such thing as "conventional warfare". That will be the beginning of the end of world as we know it. It will be important to have a Commander-in-Chief who understands how to respond to any threat.

Many members of Congress have law degrees but legislation always seems to contain loopholes. Also it seems that members of Congress do not change their minds on a legislative votes as a result of the debates on the floors of Congress. Do members of Congress consider working for lobbyists after serving in Congress? How does that influence their votes?

Crimes should be prosecuted. If there is no prosecution for breaking laws, then the crimes will continue. For example, the U. S. Government Accountability Office (GAO) makes periodic reports such as the one where it was reported of significant fraud relative to the Affordable Care Act. But there is never any report as to prosecutions of these fraud cases!

The **Selective Service System** is an independent agency of the United States government that maintains information on those potentially subject to military conscription. All male U.S. citizens and male immigrant non-citizens between the ages of 18 and 25 are required by law to have registered within 30 days of their 18th birthdays. The GAO periodically exams compliance with these requirements, but here again, there is no record of prosecutions for those who do not comply with the law.

Prosecutions, including those of the Internal Revenue Service (IRS), have the effect of deterring further non-compliance with the laws if they are reported in the news.

Federal drug laws are not enforced, and some States have legalized drugs such as marijuana for medical or recreational use! Marijuana is much more addictive than nicotine; thus more smoking, more cancer, more cost; Marijuana affects the brain and memory functions; legalized marijuana will increase the illegal use of more dangerous drugs; when a substantial number of Americans are addicted to marijuana and other drugs, national security is at risk because fewer Americans would qualify to serve in the military; the use of marijuana will drastically increase health costs. Why have prescription drugs when one can obtain these dangerous drugs by means of electronic cigarettes or on the street.

Our national borders are not secure and the whole world knows it! And the current refugee resettlement system crushes local communities economically and opens doors to possible **radical persons who have no desire to assimilate** but may be **working to harm our citizens or destroy our cherished freedoms.** Even worse, the current system often refers the important task of background checks and other interviews to unaccountable third-party groups that are more interested in the number of refugees they can process than in ensuring that those entering our country don't harbor radical tendencies.

Congress has not passed a budget in several years and keeps borrowing money and raises the national debt limit. Near election time, Congress scrambles to pass more give-away programs to lure voters for their re-election. Such irresponsible actions will soon cause a crisis when the interest on the debt is unsustainable. A Term Limit Constitutional Amendment is needed. Mark Twain noted:

"Politicians and diapers must be changed often, and for the same reason"!

Mail-in ballots is growing in popularity, mainly because government officials do not want to bother preparing for elections, and they cite the need to have greater voter turn-out. I questioned the procedures: authentication of the ballots, ballot counting procedures, knowledge that your ballot was received and counted, how to maintain a "secret ballot", who is actually voting, the mechanisms in place for countering fraud, and the security of ballots in the postal system.

Twenty-nine States have approved the call for a Constitutional Convention for the purported purpose of approving a Balanced Budget Amendment. Thirty-four states are required to call for a Convention. These State Legislators and the news media have not reviewed such an amendment. They are in favor of a "balanced budget amendment" **because it sounds good to the electorate! Same old story: "pass it so we can see what is in it". These amendments are flawed:** (1) they do not budget for paying off the national debt, (2) the debt limit is allowed to increase, (3) many exclude all courts to rule with regard to certain provisions, including the Supreme Court, (4) some would not take effect until five years after ratification, 5) many loophole phrases such as "estimates", "congress may waive", "unless", and "except", 6) at least one proposed amendment uses the phrase "duly chosen and sworn members of each house of Congress" several times, unlike the language in Constitution and is equivalent of saying "*the anointed*" and is offensive), 7) **an amendment cannot force Congress to pass a balanced budget, or any legislation**, and 8) there is no provision for consequences if a balanced budget were not passed by Congress, such as an immediate 20% decrease in federal spending.

If Congress could not agree on a balanced budget, it would be another example of Congress ignoring the Constitution. These proposed budget amendments would change the nature of the constitution from one providing organization, rights, and parameters, to one that specifies passage of certain legislation. The politicians who propose these "balanced budget amendments" should spend more time trying to legislate a budget. **A "budget amendment" will not work and is not needed.**

As time went on, I became more frustrated with all politicians. **Greed, dishonesty, egos, re-election schemes, etc. are killing our Republic.**

The TV programming is another source of frustration. The major news channels keep repeating the same news all day, and they say that it is "Breaking News" (instead of "News Update") when the news is five or six days old, or even longer! I am ready to stop TV service. I think there is a market for smart programming. For example: a news segment that reports ONLY the news with no opinions; another segment that includes news & opinion; an afternoon education segment for young school children (after school, at about 4:00 pm) that includes geography, history (U. S. & world) presented in a manner suitable for children; a segment of the "good" news of people (there is too much bad news that the mentally deranged people start wanting to do bad things; and other segments ideas that can be implemented with the proper study. The number of news "anchors is alarming, especially when I am paying too much for

TV now, viewing many more commercials than ever before. I would rather have some of these "anchors" out observing what our government is doing or not doing, i.e. finding new "breaking news" stories. The news gets boring hearing the same crap all day and night.

The news media is not fair to political candidates; they pick their favorites and feature them almost continually. Once a candidate announces a campaign, there should be equal time for all of the candidates; financial donations for political candidates should also be regulated. **If there is a problem with any Supreme Court decision regarding these matters or others, the decision can be overruled by a Constitutional Amendment!**

There are striking differences in the top news stories presented on web sites such as www.foxnew.com and www.cnn.com, etc. The difference in the top news stories is interesting and informative!

Lawyer ethics have changed! There are multiple TV Ads on all channels suggesting that the insurance industry is dishonest. Most of their settlements are secret, as well as their earnings. These Ads are at a rate of three or four per each half hour time segment, especially on Sunday mornings. Also lawyers are introducing many more frivolous law suits. All the laws governing law suits favor the lawyers.

I have found a few weaknesses in the U. S. Constitution and have discussed some of these along with proposed amendments below. None of these proposed amendments will occur unless there is a national movement to get it done. (These proposed Amendments are revised and expanded from those in the books, "Can We? - Comments and Recommendations for Preserving Our Nation" by Grant Rees and "The Liberty Amendments" by Mark Levin.)

1. Convention Method

The Constitution provides four paths for amending the U. S. Constitution per Article V: (1) Proposal by Congress, ratification by state conventions (**used once**), (2) Proposal by Congress, ratification by state legislatures (**used all other times**), (3) Proposal by convention of states, ratification by state conventions (**never used**), and (4) Proposal by convention of states, ratification by state legislatures (**never used**). (Ref: Wikipedia)

The make-up and organization of a Convention not defined in the Constitution, thus, a convention could last for many months, and propose other amendments such that the nation would be in constant turmoil for months.

The Convention method must be replaced with a safer alternative such that the State Legislatures would propose amendments to the Constitution and thus preserve State's rights to change the constitution. If Congress does not act to replace the Convention Method, there will be a Constitutional Convention called and it could get ugly.

Proposed "Replace Convention Method Amendment":

Section 1. The Convention method of amending or ratifying a proposed Amendment is hereby rescinded.

Section 2. Article V is revised as "The Congress, whenever two-thirds of both Houses shall deem it necessary, shall propose Amendments to this Constitution, or, two-thirds of the State Legislatures propose Amendments to this Constitution, which, in either case, shall be valid for all Intents and Purposes, as Part of this Constitution, when ratified by the Legislatures of three-fourths of the several States".

Section 3. An amendment proposed by the State Legislatures shall be identical in all respects relative to title and wording. After an amendment is approved by a State Legislature, a State-certified copy shall be forwarded to the Archivist of the United States. The first State to propose an amendment shall forward an exact copy to the other State Legislatures for consideration.

Section 4. A six-year time limit shall be placed on each proposed Amendment, starting from the date the said Amendment is first approved by a State Legislature. During this time limit, a State legislature may not rescind or modify the Amendment after once approved.

Section 5. After the required two-thirds of the State Legislatures have approved a proposed Amendment, as certified by the Archivist of the United States, it is then sent to the States for ratification by three-fourths of the States.

Section 6. If the amendment is proposed by the State Legislatures, the subsequent ratification shall be a separate approval vote, even if a State was one that proposed or approved the Amendment.

Section 7. This article shall take effect immediately after being ratified.

2. Term Limits

Some believe that "Term Limits for Congress" should be decided at the ballot box; however, many party leaders discourage competition in the primary elections, citing seniority; thus the same persons running in order to preserve seniority for powerful chairmanship positions, and they become more receptive to the lobbyists than the electorate. Furthermore the longer they serve the more they are tempted by the many vices of mankind. There are hundreds of ex-members of Congress who have been indicted for various crimes, some still in prison.

Proposed "Term Limits Amendment":

Section 1. A person may be elected to the U. S. House of Representatives a maximum of eight two-year terms, except as provided in Section 3.

Section 2. A person may be elected to the U. S. Senate a maximum of three six-year terms, except as provided in Section 3

Section 3. No person may serve more than 32 years of combined service as a Representative and Senator, and shall be ineligible to be on a ballot if this limit of service is met before the end of the term of office.

Section 4. Seniority in the House or Senate is based only on the time served in the respective house of Congress.

Section 5. This article shall take effect 120 days after being ratified as an amendment to the Constitution within seven years from the day of its submission to the States by the Congress. Upon ratification, those incumbents in the House and Senate who have exceeded their limits of service shall complete their current term of office.

3. U.S. Supreme Court

The U. S. Constitution does not establish requirements for the Chief Justice and the Associate Justices, regarding age, citizenship, experience, etc., nor does it specify the size of the court. President Franklin D. Roosevelt tried to "stack" the court with fifteen justices, but his Judicial Procedure Reform Bill of 1937 was defeated. Thus the size of the court has remained at nine justices per the Judiciary Act of 1869. The court has been accused of "legislating from the bench". **If a ruling appears to be very unpopular, a Supreme Court ruling can be overturned by amending the Constitution!**

Proposed "Supreme Court Amendment":

Section 1. The United States Supreme Court shall consist of one Chief Justice and eight associate Justices. They shall be nominated by the President and confirmed by the Senate per Article II, Section 2 of the Constitution.

Section 2. A person nominated for the Supreme Court must be a natural born citizen of the United States, and has lived in the United States a minimum of 30 years. The nominee must be at least 45 years of age, and must have been a judge for a minimum of four years.

Section 3. A United States Supreme Court justice shall not serve longer than 30 years, but shall not apply to justices who are serving at the time of ratification of this amendment.

Section 4. This article shall be inoperative unless it shall have been ratified as an amendment to the Constitution by the legislatures of three-fourths of the several states within seven years from the day of its submission to the states by the Congress.

4. Election of Senators

When the U. S. Constitution was ratified, Section 3 of Article I stated that two Senators from each State would be chosen by the State Legislators. The 17th Amendment changed this procedure in 1913 by specifying that Senators would be elected by the people of the various States. However, the influence of out-of-State money, and other factors, has made this procedure unfair. The 17th amendment should be rescinded.

Proposed "Selecting U.S. Senator By State Legislatures" Amendment

Section 1. The Seventeenth Amendment is hereby repealed. All Senators shall be chosen by their respective State Legislatures as originally specified.

Section 2. All Senators who are serving at the time of ratification of this amendment shall continue to serve their current term.

Section 3. A Senator may be removed from office by a two-thirds vote of the State legislature, or be expelled per section 5 of Article I.

Section 4. When vacancies happen in the representation of any State in the Senate, the legislature of the State may empower the executive thereof to make temporary appointments until the legislature may select a Senator.

Section 5. This article shall be inoperative unless it shall have been ratified as an amendment to the Constitution by the legislatures of three-fourths of the several states within seven years from the day of its submission to the states by the Congress.

CHAPTER THIRTEEN

REVIEW OF MEDICAL OBSERVATIONS

THE FOLLOWING SUMMARIZES SHIRLEY'S AND my medical events:

1. I was diagnosed with Pulmonary Fibrosis in 2010 and learned that mean life expectancy of 2.8 years from the time of the diagnosis, or the upper limit of life expectancy is five years. I learned that drugs prescribed have serious side affects and the benefits don't seem to outweigh the risks. I opted not to take the prescribed drugs.

2. I also learned in 2010 that one of the nerves to my diaphragm was severed during my neck surgery in 2003. I was never told of this problem and the potential risks of a neck injury that could end my life.

3. Universities seek participants for various cancer studies, but don't follow up with the patients who do not participate. Some of the studies were stopped because of increased deaths or serious side affects. Universities seem to be more interested in research dollars than in finding cures.

4. I believe that my wife's doctor prescribed an excess number of tests: colonoscopy, upper GI endoscopy, and Virtual colonoscopy the same day; and the next day a CT scan

was scheduled, and five days later a PET scan. The virtual colonoscopy and a CT scan were done without doctor in the facility and these tests hurt my wife and caused pain, discomfort, nausea, and stomach blockages for many months. These excess tests were likely prescribed for profit rather than for the patient's best interest. Also since her system was upset, it is likely the reason that the chemo treatments resulted in being hospitalized. As we had good insurance coverage, this appears to have influenced the excessive number of tests.

5. At one of the nursing/rehab facilities the nurse attending my wife demonstrated unclean procedures: picking up Shirley's food and medications in her bare hands.

6. This same nurse gave my wife a dangerous drug, seroquel, which was not prescribed by Shirley's doctor, and very likely was given to other patients as well. Nurses should not be giving dangerous medications without a doctor's orders, and medicatioins given should be recorded.

7. It appears that Nurses are keeping left-over medications from discharged patients in their personal drawers.

8. Nurses are working nominal 12 hour shifts which extend to two or three more hours because of shift turn-over procedures. Some nurses are working double-shifts with very little sleep during which time the patients are not properly attended to. Also nurses are working while pregnant. Some medical personnel work long hours at more than one medical facility (hospital; nursing home, etc.)

9. During Shirley's lengthy stay in the hospital following her colon surgery, she was given three or four antibiotics at a time. After researching some more, I learned that the administration of excessive number of antibiotics, simultaneously, while in the hospital can cause C. diff. Sure enough, Shirley got the C. diff

bacteria. I also learned that on February 8, 2012, the U.S. Food and Drug Administration (FDA) informed the public that the use of stomach acid drugs known as proton pump inhibitors (PPIs), such as Omeprazole (prilosec) may be associated with an increased risk of C. diff and recommended that a diagnosis of C. diff be considered for patients taking PPIs who develop diarrhea that does not improve.

10. Signiicant difference between images of the first and second upper GI endoscopy shows damage to Shirley's digestive lining, most likely from the Virtual Colonoscopy.

11. Chemo Therapy was started too soon, as evidenced by blood tests. Shirley was too weak. The oncologist had intended to use the drug avastin, and when it was learned that he was not using it, the oncologist admitted that chemo was too soon after surgery to use it. This caused her to be admitted to the hospital twice. The results of the blood tests prior to administering chemo were not available until after the drugs were administered. The results seemed to indicate that Chemo should not have been given. Also, one never knows what drugs the patient is receiving when receiving them intravenously.

12. The number of drugs keeps increasing, and no evidence that doctors re-evaluate the need to continue some of the medications.

13. Errors in prescriptions: "Take two tablets twice daily" (i.e. total of four pills a day) when it was meant to say "Take one tablet twice daily" (i.e. total of two pills a day); and when a prescription is renewed and they don't have the correct dosage, so substitute a pill with double dosage with the instructions to take a half pill. For a refill, the patient might not look at the change of instructions on the bottle.

14. When Shirley went for a second opinion on her treatments, the doctors were more interested in her participating in a university study than offering any treatment suggestions.

15. The Power port which was installed in Shirley's chest when she had surgery was plugged. This is a indication of improper maintenance of the device. This resulted in having a "pick line" installed in her arm which had to be carefully covered to prevent infection – a high maintenance item for the patient.

16. As we were inquiring various options with our local oncologist for further cancer treatments, two suggestions were made that did not involve chemo therapy drugs: infusion of erbitux or take a daily pill, stivarga. We learned that the ratail cost of the pill was $23,000 for each 84 pill order. We were wondering why the doctor would opt for the pill, stivarga, rather than the weekly infusion of erbitux. With infusion the doctor could charge for services. Then we thought that the drug company might be compensating the doctor for prescribing the pill.

17. We learned that the manufacturer of the pill, stivarga, recommends a blood test to check liver function. The oncologist did not mention any preliminary blood tests or on-going blood tests for Stivarga! His staff told Shirley that we would not have to pay the rest of our $1,000 deductible to the mail-order pharmacy!

18. It has been nearly five years since my diagnosis of Pulmonary Fibrosis and I have been feeling good. I frequently wonder if the Pulmonary Fibrosis diagnosis was correct. My doctors have not ordered another X-ray or other tests to check on progress of the disease. In an earlier chapter I talked about university research in that is was mostly a statistical study rather than a basic research study. You would think that all the doctors with patients who have the disease would receive brief updates on

research findings so that they could pass the information on to their patients.

19. It appears that none of the cancer treatments were effective for Shirley for one reason or another (stomach blockages, internal damage that may have been caused by the virtual colonoscopy).

20. Changing doctors is difficult because hospital corporate policy does not allow a change of doctors within the corporation, at least those in the same office complex. With many doctors grouping together to save overhead costs, this makes it impossible for a patient to choose a doctor to his or her liking.

21. There seems to be evidence that gratuities or payments are made to doctors from the hospital corporation for referring other specialists within the corporation?

22. There also appears that gratuities or payments, kickbacks, etc. are given to doctors by drug companies for prescribing their medications? There may be conflicts of interest when a doctor becomes a "Study Doctor" for a university.

23. There appears to be no oversight of the medical profession. If there are problems or law suits, they are kept secret. The lawyers are always the winners, the public is the loser: --- higher insurance premiums in order to pay the lawyers.

24. When a patient leaves the hospital, nursing home, or rehab facility, how are left-over drugs disposed of?

25. If there were a cure for various cancers discovered, a lot of medical staffs would be out of work. Is there any incentive for finding cures for diseases and medical problems? I suspect that any solution might come from another country and Americans will go out of country for the cure! I think our country spends too

much money for trials and statistical studies on existing drugs and not enough for basic research for finding cures for diseases.

26. When one is undergoing chemo treatments, could an oncologist weaken the dose so as to have the patient continue to come for treatments? Is the object of treatments to obtain remission of the disease or to profit the doctors by having the patients treated for longer periods of time?

27. During the time I was a caregiver for Shirley, an X-ray indicated that I had pneumonia. The doctor then prescribed 500 mg amoxicillin capsules. The prescription read: "Take two capsules by mouth three times a day for 10 days". This was 3,000 mg each day. A reputable website recommended dosage for a 500 mg pill was 3 times a day or twice a day for a 875 mg pill, to be administered for 7 to 10 days (thus 1500 mg or 1750 mg a day) which is about half of what was prescribed for me!

28. I have learned that one has to check on the medications prescribed. I had to get a new primary care doctor since the previous one was moving out of the area. After my first visit with multiple blood tests, etc., the doctor's nurse called me to tell me that the doctor wants me to discontinue Januvia (for type 2 diabetes) because "it was too expensive", and wanted me to take Actos. I responded that I had been taking Januvia for several years and have had no problem, and wanted to think about it. With the experience that I have had with Shirley's care, I wanted to research the drug and add it to the nearly 100 files I had created in a folder I call "Medical Information".

After researching this drug I found that "multiple medical studies link the Type 2 diabetes medication Actos to the onset of bladder cancer. The drug maker, in April 2015, "settled about 9,000 Actos-relative lawsuits for $2.37 billion"! I won't be taking this drug. I thought again whether the drug companies are compensating doctors for prescribing their drugs which should be illegal.

29. There should be a place where a patient can register a complaint so that noted problems or concerns can be addressed. If there is such a place, it must be more evident. If one sees gross negligence or malpractice, the problem will continue to exist unless some action is taken. I would rather the medical profession take correct these problems rather than the legal system.

30. The discussions of choosing a doctor might not apply in the near future. More and more government control of medical practices will eventually leave the patient with no choice as the doctors will likely be assigned. A socialist state will always make sure that all doctors have the same number of patients, regardless of their skill level.

31. Shirley never completed her prescribed chemo treatments because the initial dosages resulted in her hospitalization.

Despite some my experiences with the medical profession, I recognize that there have been amazing advances in medical technology, surgeries, medicines, and treatment methodologies. But one has to be adequately informed of the risks vs benefits for various medical procedures and treatments. I am grateful that the United States has some of the best doctors, treatments, facilities, and drugs in the world.

CHAPTER FOURTEEN

A REMARKABLE LADY AND THE FUTURE

ON JUNE 18, 2015 SHIRLEY passed away after having been admitted to a hospice facility the night before. It has been twenty months since she had Colon surgery. During this time she was in the hospital four times and nursing/rehab facilities three times. She was constantly going to medical facilities for doctor appointments, removing ports, installing a pick line, installing a new port, CT Scans, X-rays, ProTime checks of her blood, recovery, cancer treatments, etc.

For the last few months of Shirley's life, she felt pressure around her belt line, and her legs and ankles were swollen. As a result of taking nausea and pain pills frequently she was sleeping, or nearly asleep all day. She was progressively getting weaker and had difficulty getting up the three steps from the garage to the house and was again using a walker in the house. Her appetite diminished greatly.

I have been blessed with a remarkable lady as my wife for 54-1/2 years, and I was blessed to be able to care for Shirley. She was a real fighter for her life. She was everybody's friend. She loved her family. The last twenty months of caring for her was a small measure of pay-back for the many years that she took care of her family. It also turns out to be a blessing that I did not participate in one of the university studies that caused many fatalities, thus I was able to care for Shirley.

I am comforted by the memories of a caring wife, mother, grandmother, and friend to all.

Shirley, in June 2014, one year before she died. This was during a nine months period when she had no treatments.

It is very difficult to contemplate the future of America, the United States. The political system is becoming more corrupt every day, and the "free press" is doing a lousy job. Religion is being mocked, attacked, and ridiculed. Ethics and honesty are becoming obsolete. I feel little hope for our posterity. The United States needs a miracle in the 2016 elections.

When I see a baby or a child, I wonder what the world will look like when he or she obtains my age!

ABOUT THE AUTHOR

Grant Rees is a retired engineer who now writes political letters and commentary. He published a book in 2011, "Can We? Comments and Recommendations for Preserving Our Nation". He is a fiscal conservative and desires that Congress legislate a meaningful budget with a plan to repay the national debt. He serves in his church and volunteers for community service. Grant was raised in Reno, Nevada and after graduating from Reno High School, he attended the U. S. Naval Academy and served a career in the Navy, including a tour in Vietnam. He earned three degrees: BS, USNA, Annapolis 1959; a MSEE, Naval Postgraduate School, Monterey, CA, 1966; and MBA, American Univ., Washington, DC 1978. After his military service he worked as an engineer for Argonne National Laboratory at their facility outside of Idaho Falls, Idaho. Grant has resided in Nevada, on Navy Ships, California, Vietnam, Oregon, Maryland, Idaho, and Utah. He and his wife of 54-1/2 years had two sons.

Printed in the United States
By Bookmasters